Seeing Ourselves Through God's Eyes

By
Teresa Colón

ISBN: 978-1-7322925-0-5 (eBook)
ISBN: 978-0-692-11414-8 (Paperback)

Library of Congress Control Number: 2018942571

Although the author and publisher have made every effort to ensure that the information in this book was correct at press time, the author and publisher do not assume and hereby disclaim any liability to any party for any loss, damage, or disruption caused by errors or omissions, whether such errors or omissions result from negligence, accident, or any other cause. Some names and identifying details have been changed to protect the privacy of individuals.

This book is not intended as a substitute for the medical advice of physicians. The reader should regularly consult a physician in matters relating to his/her health and particularly with respect to any symptoms that may require diagnosis or medical attention.

Additional Credits:
Front cover image by lightwise © 123rf.com
Book design by Crystal Prairie Media and Nate Brochin
Scripture quotations are from THE HOLY BIBLE, NEW INTERNATIONAL VERSION®, NIV® Copyright © 1973, 1978, 1984, 2011 by Biblica, Inc.® Used by permission. All rights reserved worldwide.

Published by Crystal Prairie Media LLC, in the United States of America.
First printing edition 2018.

Contents

Foreword

I've struggled with mental illness most of my life, although I was unaware of it. I've been diagnosed with General Anxiety Disorder (July 2010), Depression (March 2016), and then had both of those diagnoses amended to the more appropriate diagnosis of Bipolar Disorder II (October 2016).

It wasn't until the depression diagnosis that I finally started to take my situation seriously and do the work needed to start healing. It hasn't been easy and it has been deeply rewarding.

As I continued my journey to mental health, I started leading peer groups for Christians living with mental illnesses, using a great curriculum offered by the Mental Health Grace Alliance. In doing so, I discovered that many of the faith issues I struggled with were not unique to me and that many of the answers I'd received from my Christian family were not Biblically accurate.

My disorder is not a sign of my sin or demon possession; it is a mark that I am claimed by God to do some higher work. It is the thorn in my side that troubles me and motivates me.

I want to help you see for yourself that it is OK to be unwell; God loves you anyway. I have several prayers for you as you make your way through this devotional:

- That you may see that your experiences are also reflected in the Bible. You are not the first to have these feelings and you are not alone in them.
- That you may get some truth behind what a mental illness is (an illness) and isn't (a sign of sin or worse).
- That you will know that God loves you and claims you for who you are. He knows you better than you know yourself, and it is exactly what he loves about you.
- That you will know that this season may be dark and terrible - and also, temporary. We have seasons of depression, or anxiety, or mood cycles, but we will have seasons of calm.
- Most importantly, that you are made for a purpose beyond this one experience. You have a place in the family we both belong to: God's family, the Body of Christ. We each have a role to play and an important contribution to make; this season doesn't change those facts. You are wanted and loved by the Body as you are by the Father, and we need what you have to offer.

Father, I ask that you walk with my brothers and sisters in Christ as they work their way through this devotional. Help them, Father, to experience the unbound love you offer us. Help them to see the value you place on their life, a value beyond counting. Lord, I also ask that you help relieve the pain and suffering our family may be going through. Grant your peace and help walk them back to a place of safety and stability.

In Jesus' name, I pray. Amen.

One last thought before you get started...if you have a question, have a revelation you want to share, or just want me to include you specifically in my prayers, I encourage you to email me at teresa@woundedbirdsministry.com. I respond to all emails (sometimes it takes me a couple days) and I love hearing from you!

Week 1:

You Are God's Beloved

Overview

In the worst of the storm, we can feel unloved and worse, unlovable. It can be hard to remember that God loves us for who we are, no matter what we've done. In fact, not only does he love us, he designed and created us out of his deep love! This week, we'll remind ourselves that we are God's beloved. He loves us, claims us, and celebrates our love of him - even when we can't feel his presence.

And yes - that means you, too.

Day 1: You Are Loved

Devotional

When in a depression, it is common to feel as though God has retreated or abandoned us. It can be scary and makes us feel unloved and unlovable. In these Scriptures, God reminds us not only that he loves us but that he is close to us in the depths of our pain, even when we can't sense his presence.

Like a tall tree whose upper branches can't always be seen from the ground, he is our safe shelter. He protects us even when we can't see it.

Reading

Psalm 34:18
The Lord is close to the brokenhearted
and saves those who are crushed in spirit.

Psalm 36:7
How priceless is your unfailing love, O God!
People take refuge in the shadow of your wings.

Prayer

Lord, I am scared, sad, and uncomfortable. Thank you for being my refuge, for staying close to me even when I don't feel it. Please help me see the reminders that I am loved not just by you, but by others, as well. Amen.

Teresa's Notes

Today's message is often one of the toughest to believe, and I know that because I've been there. As I started treating my disorder, I began to see all the little ways that God held me in the worst of my pain. I couldn't see him, couldn't feel him, and often didn't want him there, and yet I know now he still loved and sheltered me through it all.

Personal Response

What does it mean to you to know that God is close and watching over you, even when you can't sense him?

Spend some time today looking for little signs of love. These can be as simple as noticing someone opening a door for you or offering you to bring you a cup of tea. At the end of the day, write down two acts of love you experienced.

Day 2: You Are Worthy

Devotional

The story of Zacchaeus is an encouraging one for anyone who feels unlovable. As a tax collector, he commonly extorted taxpayers, making him a hated and despised man. He was considered sinful, terrible, and unfit for society.

Jesus, however, did not agree. He knew that Zacchaeus had done terrible things, and also that Zacchaeus was worthy of Christ's love. Without hesitation, he reaches out to Zacchaeus and includes him - even greeting Zacchaeus "warmly."

No matter what we've done or the ways in which we've let down our family, friends, or ourselves, Jesus considers us worthy of his friendship and love. We are not perfect and never can be perfect; Jesus knows this and loves us anyway. Our worth is not determined by our actions or how society views us, but by the love and friendship Jesus offers us.

Reading

Luke 19:1-10

^{1}Jesus entered Jericho and was passing through. ^{2}A man was there by the name of Zacchaeus; he was a chief tax collector and was wealthy. ^{3}He wanted to see who Jesus was, but because he was short he could not see over the crowd. ^{4}So he ran ahead and climbed a sycamore-fig tree to see him, since Jesus was coming that way.

^{5}When Jesus reached the spot, he looked up and said to him, "Zacchaeus, come down immediately. I must stay at your house today." ^{6}So he came down at once and welcomed him gladly.

Prayer

Jesus, I am overwhelmed that you consider me worthy of your friendship and your love. Often, it doesn't feel like I am worthy of even a kind word, and yet you offer me so much more. I praise you for your mercy and your love. Thank you for seeing in me what I struggle to see in myself. Amen.

Teresa's Notes

I love this story of Zaccheus, at least partially because I am so short and would have also had to climb a tree to see Jesus! As I've walked my journey back to mental health, I've had to face some uncomfortable truths. I've had to look at some of the things I've done in my life - some driven by my disorder, others not - and bring them back to the feet of Jesus. Like Zaccheus, it would be enough for me to know that I simply glimpsed Jesus, and yet he calls me into a relationship with him. Jesus decides my worthiness, not my past.

Personal Response

What does it mean to you that Jesus wants your friendship? What is your response to his warm greeting?

Day 3: You Are Designed

Devotional

Yesterday, we talked about how Jesus finds us worthy of friendship, even when we don't recognize it or think we deserve it. One of the reasons Jesus considers us worthy is that he knows how we came into being: God designed us. Nothing about us is an accident. Every cell in our body, every chemical firing (or not) in our brains is intentional. We may not understand why God made us the way he did, but he tells us that it is intentional.

Not only are we designed by God, we are "fearfully and wonderfully made." We know that all his "works are wonderful," and those works include you! He made you for a purpose. There is a plan for us and the pain we are in is part of that plan. We may not understand why he gave us the path he did, but we can take comfort in knowing that all God's creation is beautiful and amazing and we are part of his larger creation.

Reading

Psalm 139:1-4

¹³For you created my inmost being;
    you knit me together in my mother's womb.

¹⁴I praise you because I am fearfully and
wonderfully made;
    your works are wonderful,
    I know that full well.

¹⁵My frame was not hidden from you
    when I was made in the secret place,
    when I was woven together in the depths of the
earth.

¹⁶Your eyes saw my unformed body;
    all the days ordained for me were written in your
book
    before one of them came to be.

Prayer

Father, all your creations are wonderful, and I know that includes me. As much as I can read that in your word, sometimes it is still hard to believe. Yet, as I read your words I am reminded that I was designed and created in love, in your perfect love. Lord, I don't understand why I'm in this season of life, but I trust that it fills the purpose for which you designed me. Thank you for the care you showed in creating me, and for loving me so much that you made me. Amen.

Teresa's Notes

Today's reading is one I've struggled with. If God made me so wonderfully, then why have I made so many mistakes? While there are no clear answers, I think there is a measure of grace: my mistakes have made me into the woman who could accept Christ's love and sacrifice, and give me a place from which I can reach out to others in the same pain I've lived through.

Personal Response

Do you feel "fearfully and wonderfully made"? What are some reasons you struggle to remember that?

What does it mean to you to know that God designed you on purpose and for a purpose?

Day 4: You Are Known

Devotional

It can be easy to think that God doesn't want to know us, and the truth is that he knows us better than we know ourselves. Even when he feels distant from us, he is everywhere and knows everything - including our thoughts, our feelings, our pain and despair, our longings, and our faith.

He knows our doubts; he knows our sin; he knows our love.

He loves us when we have unkind thoughts and he loves us when we praise him. He knows when we are struggling and he knows when we achieve. He knows the greatness we are capable of, and he knows the lessons we need to learn to unlock that greatness.

As we walk the road to mental health, often the process includes us getting to know ourselves better. What experiences upset or trigger us? What are our responses to stressful situations? How can we be more mindful? How can we live in a healthier way?

God already knows the answers to all those questions. He knows us better than we know ourselves, and we can trust the Holy Spirit to provide us with insight and wisdom.

Reading

Psalm 139:1-4

[1]You have searched me, Lord,
and you know me.

[2]You know when I sit and when I rise;
you perceive my thoughts from afar.

[3]You discern my going out and my lying down;
you are familiar with all my ways.

[4]Before a word is on my tongue
you, Lord, know it completely.

Prayer

Lord, you made me and know me so well. Help me to learn myself as well as you know me. Guide me in the process of uncovering more of who I am and who you made me to be. I praise you, Lord, for your kindness, your gentleness, and your unconditional love. Amen.

Teresa's Notes

Today's reading is a blessing and a struggle for me. It is wonderful to know that I have no secrets from God and that he loves me for who I am. One blessing in this reading for me is that when I have come across a situation in therapy that I decided needed prayer, there was no shame in bringing to God: he already knew it. He already knew the details of it. It was important for my relationship with him that I say the words and be honest about my motivations, but none of it is a surprise to him!

It makes me think of my daughter; when she was a little kid, she would sometimes play with my makeup and make a mess. I would call her to it and ask her about it. She would always try to duck it at first ("the fish did that, Mom!"), but eventually she would admit it. I already knew the truth, but it was still important that she acknowledge her own error. It didn't change my love for her, not at all.

God knows me better than I know myself and sometimes, I just have to acknowledge that truth.

Personal Response

What is one thing you are learning about yourself? What is your response to learning this?

What does it mean to you that God already knew this about you, and loves and accepts you just as you are?

Day 5: You Are Desired

Devotional

God not only loves us, he desires us beyond words. Sometimes, we wander off and get lost. When this happens, he works hard to bring us back into the flock. He rejoices when we turn to him.

Rather than condemning the sheep for getting lost, Jesus tells us only the joy the shepherd feels over the sheep rejoining the flock.

In the same way, Jesus tells us God celebrates us every time we make the decision to turn towards him. There is no need or place for guilt in this moment. After all, does the lost sheep feel guilt over being lost? Or fearful while lost and then feel joy and safety when found? We are invited to share in the joy of our relationship with God, whose desire for us exceeds imagination.

Reading

Luke 15:3-7

[3]Then Jesus told them this parable: [4]"Suppose one of you has a hundred sheep and loses one of them. Doesn't he leave the ninety-nine in the open country and go after the lost sheep until he finds it? [5]And when he finds it, he joyfully puts it on his shoulders [6]and goes home. Then he calls his friends and neighbors together and says, 'Rejoice with me; I have found my lost sheep.' [7]I tell you that in the same way there will be more rejoicing in heaven over one sinner who repents than over ninety-nine righteous persons who do not need to repent.

Prayer

Lord, sometimes I forget how much you desire me. It doesn't seem possible on the days when I feel low and unworthy, yet you tell me how much you desire me in your Word. Help me keep my mind and my heart turned toward you, Lord. I rejoice in our relationship and in your deep love for me. Amen.

Teresa's Notes

This is one of my favorite readings because it reminds me that Jesus searched for and pursued me across my life. I'm stubborn, so he really had to fight for me. It wasn't until I really felt my brokenness that I realized that if I wanted a different life, I needed to stop doing things my way because my way wasn't working. That was the moment that Jesus found me and I joined his flock for good.

Personal Response

What is one time you have wandered away from God? What brought you back?

What does it mean to you to know that God celebrated your return with joy?

Day 6: You Are Claimed

Devotional

"Do not fear, for I have redeemed you; / I have summoned you by name; you are mine."
(Isaiah 43:1)

With these words in Isaiah, God reminds us that he claims us. When we claim something, we declare possession or ownership over it. We put our name on it and care for it. We place it in a special spot, a place where we can view it with pride, affection, and many other wonderful emotions.

It's the same in a marriage ceremony: each spouse claims the other. "She is MY wife." "He is MY husband." Newlyweds rejoice in saying "my husband" and "my wife" to others in conversation; it gives a sense of belonging to something (a marriage) - and someone (our spouse and family) - greater than us.

In this same way, God reminds us that he summons each of us. In the summoning and in the claiming, he declares his love for us on a new level. He reminds us that he is with us in our darkest of nights, in the worst of our storms. Though we may not see him, he is always walking with us. Though we may not feel it, he shields us from the worst of the damage.

He claims us. He claims YOU. Doesn't that feel good?

Reading

Isaiah 43:1

¹But now, this is what the Lord says -
he who created you, Jacob,
he who formed you, Israel:
"Do not fear, for I have redeemed you;
I have summoned you by name; you are mine.

²When you pass through the waters,
I will be with you;
and when you pass through the rivers,
they will not sweep over you.
When you walk through the fire,
you will not be burned;
the flames will not set you ablaze.

³ᵃFor I am the Lord your God,
the Holy One of Israel, your Savior;

Prayer

Father, I am overwhelmed by you. You summoned me and called me yours. You claim me, Lord. You are not ashamed of me or whom I am, even knowing all I am and all I've done. Lord, thank you for calling me and offering me your protection. I rejoice in your love. Amen.

Teresa's Notes

This reading is one of my all-time favorites. When I first received my diagnosis of bipolar disorder, I spent some time wrestling with my faith. Is it real, or is it simply a chemical reaction in my brain? After pondering this for a while, I came to the conclusion that the answer is, "yes." I am made for faith; I am made to belong to him. My disorder is a sign that God made me to believe in him. My disorder has led me to an amazing faith and walked me through amazing grace. In his claiming, I am redeemed!

Personal Response

What does it mean to you to be claimed? Who else has claimed you in your life?

Your belief in God is not an accident. What's one way you know you were summoned by God?

Day 7: You Are Celebrated

Devotional

When we turn toward God, he is not the only one who celebrates! Jesus tells us that all the angels rejoice when we declare our love for God. In today's passage, the woman calls all her friends and neighbors to share her good news with them; the angels do the same.

We see something similar in retail outlets during the Christmas season. Merchants who fundraise for charities at their checkout process will often have the cashiers shout out or ring a bell every time someone donates; it's an opportunity for the staff and the customers to all celebrate together.

I imagine a big bell ringing in heaven every time someone turns toward God, with the sound resonating across the entire plane. Imagine how loud it rang when you made your decision! And that's just the first moment I can picture the angels giving a big shout in response, the sound of their joy dwarfing that of the bell. I don't know if that's what really happens, but Jesus tells us that the response is similar.

You are celebrated. Rejoice in it.

Reading

Luke 15:8-10

^{8}"Or suppose a woman has ten silver coins and loses one. Doesn't she light a lamp, sweep the house and search carefully until she finds it? ^{9}And when she finds it, she calls her friends and neighbors together and says, 'Rejoice with me; I have found my lost coin.' ^{10}In the same way, I tell you, there is rejoicing in the presence of the angels of God over one sinner who repents."

Prayer

Lord, it's hard to picture the joy you took in my repentance and how all the angels rejoiced when I turned to you. I take comfort in the words of Jesus and in the idea that there was rejoicing over my decision. Thank you for celebrating me, Lord!

Teresa's Notes

Anyone who knew me in my late teens or early 20s is probably surprised that I am a Christian today. I didn't persecute Christians as Paul did, but I certainly mocked them. To say I wanted nothing to do with the faith is an understatement (in fact, I only read the Bible so I could wash my hands of the faith altogether!). Becoming a Christian was, for me, the antithesis of all I thought I stood for. I am pretty confident that the heavenly clamor at my baptism was epic.

Personal Response

What do you imagine when Jesus says that the angels in heaven rejoice when someone turns toward God?

How does it make you feel to know that was the response when you first invited Jesus in as your Lord and Savior?

Week 2:

You Are Not Alone

Overview

Did you know that the Bible is full of examples of mental illnesses? Christians can get mixed messages about what mental illnesses are - and aren't - and it can be frustrating and confusing for someone trying to pray their way through dark nights and troubled days. In his generosity, God gives us many examples of mental illness, and also helps us put to rest some common myths that exist in the Christian community.

Day 8: Depression Exists in the Bible

Devotional

Too often, Christians with depression are told that their pain comes from a lack of faith. This idea is simply untrue. We see examples of depression throughout the Bible, including several times in the Psalms. When we read these passages, we are reminded that not only is depression Biblical, we have examples of how to pray through it within the Bible itself.

Reading

Psalm 6:2-7

2Have mercy on me, Lord, for I am faint;
heal me, Lord, for my bones are in agony.

3My soul is in deep anguish.
How long, Lord, how long?

4Turn, Lord, and deliver me;
save me because of your unfailing love.

5Among the dead no one proclaims your name.
Who praises you from the grave?

6I am worn out from my groaning.
All night long I flood my bed with weeping
and drench my couch with tears.

7My eyes grow weak with sorrow;
they fail because of all my foes.

Prayer

Lord, thank you for the reminder that my depression doesn't exist because I don't have enough faith or trust in you. It is hard to pray when I hurt so strongly, and I am encouraged to see how others have prayed to you in their anguish, as well. Lord, I pray that you lift this cloud from me and help me feel the comfort you offer. Amen.

Teresa's Notes

Once I had my diagnosis, my reading of the Bible shifted. In particular, Lamentations and the Psalms read differently to me. As I learned more about depression and anxiety, I began to realize that the Bible contains examples of them. It was comforting to me to know that I wasn't the first and it helped me find the words to pray on my darkest nights.

Personal Response

Have you seen other examples of depression in Bible? Are you surprised to see that the Bible includes examples of mental illness?

Does it help to know that mental illness is not new, and that people have prayed about it to God for thousands of years?

Day 9: Jesus Had Anxiety

Devotional

Too often, we emphasize Jesus' divinity and forget his humanity. It is important to remember that Jesus was capable of - and did! - experiencing the full range of human emotions, including despair and anxiety.

Jesus knew the sacrifice needed to make us right with God, and - like any rational human - it scared him! He prayed to God earnestly on the Mount of Olives. He asked God to spare Jesus the trial he knew he was going to face. In response, "an angel from heaven appeared to him and strengthened him." (Luke 22:43)

Even after this divine support was granted him, Jesus was still anxious about what laid ahead. In fact, his anxiety was so extreme that he sweated drops of blood! This condition is called "hematodrosis," and it is very rare -and typically only seen in people awaiting execution. Not only did Jesus experience anxiety, he lived it on a level that very few of us can relate to.

Reading

Luke 22:44

^{44}And being in anguish, he prayed more earnestly, and his sweat was like drops of blood falling to the ground.

Prayer

Lord, I know that you experienced anxiety, anguish, and despair, too. It helps me to know that I'm not the only one who has felt this way. Please, Father, help me feel safe. Quiet the fears in my head that keep me from sleeping at night and pursue me during the day. Grant me rest and your true peace. Amen.

Teresa's Notes

My pastor told us one Christmas that if we can't picture Jesus as a colicky and poopy baby, then we aren't genuinely appreciating his full humanity. Sometimes God calls me to do things I don't want to do, and this picture of Jesus in the Garden of Gethsemane reminds me that Jesus didn't want to do everything God asked of him either. Sweating blood is a level of anxiety I've never achieved! Yet, even with that level of fear, Jesus moved forward. His example helps me when I don't think I have the courage I need to take the next step; it reminds me that I don't need the courage, I just need the obedience.

Personal Response

Did you know that Jesus experienced anxiety? What is your response to this understanding?

Day 10: Jesus Felt Separated from God

Devotional

One common depression symptom is feeling separated from God. It feels like he has left us, retreated from us, or abandoned us. Regrettably, the Christian community is known to make this an issue of faith or sin: if you can't sense God, then "obviously" you have a faith issue or you have a sin you need to repent.

Nothing could be farther from the truth, and Jesus shows us that truth from the cross. At the moment he was made sin, he was no longer in perfect relationship with God and could no longer feel God's presence as Jesus was accustomed to. "My God, my God, why have you forsaken me?" Jesus cried out at the critical moment.

We know that God did not abandon Jesus. We know that God was with Jesus in that terrible moment, even though Jesus could not sense or experience God. God, who claims us as he claimed Jesus, does the same with us. He does not run away, retreat, or abandon us. He is there, even when he is beyond our human understanding. In fact, this is the reality of what Jesus accomplished for us on the cross: In his sacrifice, he ensured that we would never be separated from God again.

Reading

Matthew 27:45-46

[45]From noon until three in the afternoon darkness came over all the land. [46]About three in the afternoon Jesus cried out in a loud voice, *"Eli, Eli, lemasabachthani?"* (which means "My God, my God, why have you forsaken me?").

Prayer

Father, thank you for showing me that you are with me always. It's hard, Lord, when the depression takes hold and whispers lies into my ears. I know you never abandoned or left Jesus, and I know you love me as you love him. I know you are with me even when you are beyond my ability to experience you. Help me, Father, in my darkest moments, to remember how you love me and how close you are to me. Amen.

Teresa's Notes

These are words I've cried in the darkest of my despair. "Why have you forsaken me?" I used to always see it from Jesus' perspective. As I've gone through the therapeutic experience, I've realized that no loving parent would abandon their child in such a moment of need. It means that God never left me, even when I've felt like Jesus did.

Personal Response

Have you ever felt separated from God? What was that experience like?

If you were at the crucifixion, how would you comfort Jesus in that moment when he felt abandoned by God?

Now, change the wording around: these are the same words you can use to comfort yourself when you have these same moments.

Day 11: Paul Lived with a Thorn

Devotional

In his second letter to the Corinthians, Paul gets personal. He tells the Corinthians of a thorn he lives with, and how he begged God to remove it. We don't know the nature of the thorn Paul lived with; it could have been a mental illness, a chronic illness, or something else altogether. We do know that God refused to remove it. Paul describes the situation as a "torment."

When we are in the storm of a mental illness, it can feel like torment. We cry and we rage to God for mercy. Sometimes he relents. Other times, he doesn't - as he chose with Paul.

Paul's story encourages us not only because it is another example of an amazing Christian living with an incredible trial, but for his response to it. "For when I am weak, then I am strong." Some times, all we can do is lean on Christ and his power, just like Paul, and let that leaning be its own testimony of our faith.

Reading

2Corinthians 12:7b-10

^{7b}Therefore, in order to keep me from becoming conceited, I was given a thorn in my flesh, a messenger of Satan, to torment me. ^{8}Three times I pleaded with the Lord to take it away from me. ^{9}But he said to me, "My grace is sufficient for you, for my power is made perfect in weakness." Therefore I will boast all the more gladly about my weaknesses, so that Christ's power may rest on me. ^{10}That is why, for Christ's sake, I delight in weaknesses, in insults, in hardships, in persecutions, in difficulties. For when I am weak, then I am strong.

Prayer

Lord, I am grateful for Paul's example. Knowing that someone so close to you and who did such amazing work for the Body of Christ, lived in daily torment encourages me. I appreciate seeing that the apostles were human, too, with human challenges that I can relate to. Help me get to a place where, like Paul, I can boast of my weaknesses. Help me lean on you, Lord, in the worst of my pain. Help me to experience what Paul shared with us: "When I am weak, then I am strong." Amen.

Teresa's Notes

I go through waves of acceptance when it comes to my disorder. Some days I totally fine with my diagnosis and others I question why I have to live with it. Paul reminds me here that my disorder makes me human and that, while God could cure it with just a thought, somehow there is a purpose to it. I may never - and likely won't - ever understand the fullness of the purpose of it, but I can at least take comfort that it's not random and somehow he is glorified through it.

Personal Response

Do you relate to Paul's description of his thorn? How?

What do you think of God's response to Paul and the explanation for not removing it?

What's one way your weakness becomes your strength?

Day 12: Mental Illness Is Not Demon

Possession

Devotional

One of the more pervasive and damaging Christian myths is that mental illness and demon possession or demonic oppression are the same thing. They are flat-out two different experiences. I once read an article that shared the experiences of a psychiatrist who assisted with exorcisms.

Overwhelmingly, the people he was asked to diagnose had a mental illness that was properly treated through medication and other standard mental health treatment options. In rare cases, though, he did see examples of demon possession.

Demon possession, it said in the article, cannot be confused with mental illness by any trained medical professional. There are specific signs of demon possession that are looked for when evaluating patients to know that they are dealing with something beyond human understanding.

In the story of Legion, the demons are able to speak for themselves and carry on an independent conversation with Jesus. This is not schizophrenia or a split personality disorder situation; in this case, the only reasonable diagnosis is a supernatural one.

Further evidence that Jesus was right is that the man was immediately restored to himself after the demons were cast out; he was immediately in his right mind. For someone living with a mental illness, there is no magic wand that immediately heals us; it is a long road back to mental health and it involves a lot of work.

You are not demon-possessed. You have a medical issue, and one that is best treated by medical professionals, a good self-care plan, and continuing your spiritual walk.

Reading

Mark 5:1-19

[1]They went across the lake to the region of the Gerasenes. [2]When Jesus got out of the boat, a man with an impure spirit came from the tombs to meet him. [3]This man lived in the tombs, and no one could bind him anymore, not even with a chain. [4]For he had often been chained hand and foot, but he tore the chains apart and broke the irons on his feet. No one was strong enough to subdue him. [5]Night and day among the tombs and in the hills he would cry out and cut himself with stones.

⁶When he saw Jesus from a distance, he ran and fell on his knees in front of him. ⁷He shouted at the top of his voice, "What do you want with me, Jesus, Son of the Most High God? In God's name don't torture me!" ⁸For Jesus had said to him, "Come out of this man, you impure spirit!"

⁹Then Jesus asked him, "What is your name?"

"My name is Legion," he replied, "for we are many." ¹⁰And he begged Jesus again and again not to send them out of the area.

¹¹A large herd of pigs was feeding on the nearby hillside. ¹²The demons begged Jesus, "Send us among the pigs; allow us to go into them." ¹³He gave them permission, and the impure spirits came out and went into the pigs. The herd, about two thousand in number, rushed down the steep bank into the lake and were drowned.

¹⁴Those tending the pigs ran off and reported this in the town and countryside, and the people went out to see what had happened. ¹⁵When they came to Jesus, they saw the man who had been possessed by the legion of demons, sitting there, dressed and in his right mind; and they were afraid. ¹⁶Those who had seen it told the people what had happened to the demon-possessed man - and told about the pigs as well. ¹⁷Then the people began to plead with Jesus to leave their region.

¹⁸As Jesus was getting into the boat, the man who had been demon-possessed begged to go with him. ¹⁹Jesus did not let him, but said, "Go home to your own people and

tell them how much the Lord has done for you, and how he has had mercy on you."

Prayer

God, I've been afraid to admit that I might be plagued by a demon. It has scared me, Lord, to have those thoughts. Thank you for calming my fears and assuring me that I am not, and that I can have hope and faith in the earthly process. Lord, please watch over my doctors, my therapists, and me. Help us to make the best choices to help me experience your peace and your healing. Amen.

Teresa's Notes

I am lucky that no one has ever tried to tell me I'm demon-possessed. I do have a good friend whose husband was convinced she was. They had a rocky marriage due in part to her (undiagnosed) disorder. With her diagnosis, he got educated on the realities of mental illness. It didn't fix their marriage (relationships are complicated beasts) but it did open up a new level of conversation between them, and that had many positive impacts on their relationship.

Personal Response

Has anyone ever told you that mental illness is really demon possession? Did you believe them? Why?

What is your understanding now? Do you still believe that mental illness is the work of a demon?

How might you respond to someone in the future who suggested that you are demon-possessed and not sick

Day 13: God Is with Us Always

Devotional

When we are in the depths of our suffering, we often feel alone. Isolated. Cut off.

It is not a good feeling.

What many people don't know is that feeling separated from God is a common symptom of mental illness. It can feel as though he has pulled away from us out of disappointment. Even worse, some believe that God abandoned them in response to poor faith.

In reality, God is with us always, including when we don't sense him. Just like we know a friend is still our friend even when we aren't with them, God does not abandon us.

He loves you and is with you in this moment, even if it doesn't feel like it.

How do we know this? He tells us so in his Word.

Reading

Isaiah 54:10

Though the mountains be shaken
  and the hills be removed,
yet my unfailing love for you will not be shaken
  nor my covenant of peace be removed,"
  says the Lord, who has compassion on you.

Prayer

Father, my mind plays tricks on me. It tells me you have left me. I know your promises, Father, and I know your faithfulness. I know you are with me even in this moment, when it feels like you abandoned me. Strengthen my heart, Father, and help me keep this message close until I sense your presence again. Amen.

Teresa's Notes

I grew up Catholic and there was a hymn we sang nearly every Sunday that started "Though the mountains may fall/and the hills turn to dust/yet the love of the Lord will stand." At the time, it was one of my mom's favorite hymns. It didn't always feel true for me, though, especially when walking through some of my toughest moments. Now, I know how great his compassion is and that he's kept that promise to me, though I didn't always see it in the moment.

Personal Response

Has it ever felt like God left you? What did it feel like?

God promises us that he remains with us, even when we don't feel his presence. What is one way you can remind yourself that he is still near you?

Day 14: God Makes Us a Family

Devotional

Sometimes we forget that when we accept Christ we not only get a whole relationship with God, we also get a new family! Being a Christian means that we belong to the Body of Christ, a family larger than any human could ever create. We have brothers and sisters in Christ. For some of us, these are the first sibling relationships we get to experience; for others, it's an extension of our natural families. Either way, we belong to something greater than ourselves.

You are not alone.

Reading

Ephesians 2:19-22

[19]Consequently, you are no longer foreigners and strangers, but fellow citizens with God's people and also members of his household, [20]built on the foundation of the apostles and prophets, with Christ Jesus himself as the chief cornerstone. [21]In him the whole building is joined together and rises to become a holy temple in the Lord. [22]And in him you too are being built together to become a dwelling in which God lives by his Spirit.

Prayer

Father God, thank you for the gift of your love and the gift of a new family. You give me a chance to experience your love in both supernatural and human forms, Lord, and that is an incredible gift. Father, it can be hard to accept my new position. Help me to connect with your Body, to join more fully with my brothers and sisters through relationships. Shelter me as I take little steps out of my isolation and back into your glorious world. Amen.

Teresa's Notes

Like most of us living with a mental illness, I have strained family relationships. Entering my church community and learning what it means to be treated as a true family member has been overwhelming to me. It's changed my perceptions of what relationships can be, and those relationships have changed my heart. I love my birth family and appreciate them for all they are, but my Christian family is the first one I turn to now when I celebrate or feel lost. It is the biggest gift I think I've received out of my baptism.

Personal Response

Have you had siblings before? What was nice about it? What wasn't?

As part of the Body of Christ, you have a large family! Like all large families, it can be tough to know everyone well. What steps have you taken to get to know your brothers and sisters in Christ?

What is one step you can take to get to know one person in your Church family better? (Hint: Joining a small group or Bible study is often a simple and approachable step, including for those with social anxiety.)

Week 3:

Your Faith Is Enough

Overview

It can be easy to think that our circumstances are God's way of telling us that we aren't good enough and that we aren't doing enough. Not only is this not true, we hear over and again in the Bible that God knows we are human and that we can't bridge the gap to him. Instead, he reminds us that all he asks of us is our faith. This week, we will remind ourselves of this core Biblical truth and what God wants most of all is a relationship with his imperfect, human creation - you.

Day 15: We Are Saved by Grace

Devotional

Today, Paul reminds us that God's grace, granted to us through the sacrifice of his son, Jesus the Christ, is a gift. What is a gift? A true gift? At Christmas time, we often exchange gifts; we trade with each other. It is an unspoken rule that we exchange; it is rare that we give a gift with the pure intent of giving with no expectations. Yet, that is what God gives us: a gift, with no expectations. There is nothing we can trade him, nothing we can use in exchange. There is no way to balance the power relationship.

Grace is God's gift to you. "For he so loved the world that he gave his only son, that whoever believes in him should not perish but have eternal life," John tells us (John 3:16).

Grace is a gift. God's gift.

Reading

Ephesians 2:8-9

[8]For it is by grace you have been saved, through faith - and this is not from yourselves, it is the gift of God - [9]not by works, so that no one can boast.

Prayer

Father, your gift overwhelms my heart. It is a gift of such magnitude that I cannot comprehend it. I try, Father, I try, but I know that I only perceive the smallest sliver of what it is you truly offer me. Father, I want to ask you to make me worthy of your gift, and I know that I cheapen your gift in the asking. Instead, Father, I ask that you break down the barriers in my heart that keep me from truly receiving all that you offer me in love. Amen.

Teresa's Notes

I lived most of my life feeling pressure - pressure to perform, pressure to be good, pressure to meet the expectations of those around me. Even when I met the expectations, somehow I still wasn't quite enough. It was frustrating and demotivating. With God, it's not about what I do. It's about love: His love for me. There is nothing I can do that makes him love me. It takes all the pressure off me to perform and be good; it transforms my choices into expressions of love and worship rather than duty. It is such a relief to know that there is one relationship in my life that is not dependent on my ability to perform.

Personal Response

Have you ever been the recipient of a one-sided giving experience?

What holds you back from being able to receive a gift, such as a gift of love, wholly and purely?

What is your response to God's gift of grace? Think carefully here, and be honest with yourself. This isn't about what your response "should" be or you might like it to be; instead, what is your genuine, real response when you consider the true gift of grace our loving Father gives you?

Day 16: Mustard Seed Faith

Devotional

Jesus tells us plainly that God is not interested in the size of our faith. Even the smallest and least of our faith is enough for him - remember, he knows us better than we know ourselves!

For those of us living with mental illnesses (and even those who aren't!), we can feel separated from God. Maybe our church community tells us that this separation is a reflection of our lack of faith or our sin. We can take solace, then, in this reading: God doesn't demand perfect, strong, and unshakeable faith; he asks only for faith the size of a tiny mustard seed.

Beyond this point, Jesus also tells that God takes our faith and helps us grow it into something mighty. When we trust in God to take us as we are, to take our little faith, he works mighty changes in us.

Reading

Matthew 17:20

He replied, "Because you have so little faith. Truly I tell you, if you have faith as small as a mustard seed, you can say to this mountain, 'Move from here to there,' and it will move. Nothing will be impossible for you."

Mark 4:30-32

^{30}Again he said, "What shall we say the kingdom of God is like, or what parable shall we use to describe it? ^{31}It is like a mustard seed, which is the smallest of all seeds on earth. ^{32}Yet when planted, it grows and become the largest of all garden plants with such big branches that the birds can perch in its shade."

Prayer

Father, I worry that my faith is not big enough and not good enough for you. Thank you for the reminder that your concern is not the size of my faith, but simply that I have faith. Please stay close with me, Father, and help me grow my faith. All I want is to be close to you and know you better. Amen.

Teresa's Notes

Confession: Today's reading comes out of one of my support groups. I forget exactly what the topic was for the night, but one of the women mentioned this parable and that the idea of having faith that was only the size of a mustard seed helped her in her darkest moments. It was an idea that later got me through a depression.

Personal Response

Do you worry that your faith is not enough? Why?

Jesus tells us that all we need is mustard-seed-sized faith. What hope does this give you?

What is your response to these two parables of faith?

Day 17: Continue Learning about God

Devotional

When we hear about spending quiet time with God, it can be overwhelming. It is common to think we need to spend 30, 45 minutes or even an hour in the Bible and prayer. In reality, consistency is more important than the amount of time we spend.

We see this in our human relationships. Most of us prefer getting consistent, small moments of contact with our friends and family rather than long periods of time that only happen once or twice a year. In fact, evidence shows this is the best way to grow a truly intimate relationship with anyone.

Reading God's word and spending time in prayer with him - even 5-15 minutes a day - is meaningful and grows our relationship with him. God works mighty changes, even in small increments.

Reading

2 Timothy 3:14-15

^{14}But as for you, continue in what you have learned and have become convinced of, because you know those from whom you learned it, ^{15}and how from infancy you have known the Holy Scriptures, which are able to make you wise for salvation through faith in Christ Jesus.

Prayer

Father, I love spending time with you and I know it is the best way for me to grow in intimacy with you. I stand in awe of the way you use little moments of time to help grow and change my heart and work the healings that you offer your sons and daughters. Father, I want to know you better and sometimes life gets in the way. Please forgive me for the days I don't make time for you and help me change my habits so that you and I are in constant contact and communion. Amen.

Teresa's Notes

I may be the only person whose mental illness diagnosis can be directly tied back to their baptism, and yet that's the truth of my story. After my baptism, I wondered "what happens next?" and decided to make my way back through the Gospels. As I did so, I prayed that God would heal all my hurts and wounds "down to the smallest one." I didn't expect then that it would take me through my worst depression to date, that I would cry nearly weekly on my therapist's couch, and that coming through the other side would feel as good as it did. I clung to the stories of Jesus and the apostles' healings as I crossed the battlefield, and through it all, God's word gave me hope.

Personal Response

What does it mean to you that God wants a deep and personal relationship with you?

What does your daily practice look like? Do you schedule time for God every day? Why/why not?

What is one thing you can do to make sure you are spending time with God every day, even if just for a few moments? Is there anything you would change from what you already do?

Day 18: Stay in the Word

Devotional

Yesterday we talked about how God takes the smallest bit of our faith and helps us grow it. To do so, he asks us to stay in the Word, to continue reading the Bible and learning more about what he has to say about our lives. It is one of the most powerful ways in which God speaks to us and grows us.

Devotionals, like this one, are one way to stay in the Word (and can be excellent resources). As we progress on our faith journey, the closer we want to get to God's Word, and there is no better way to do so than to get directly into the Bible.

However we choose to approach our relationship with God, consistency is the biggest factor. Each time we open his Word, we demonstrate our love for him and our desire for a stronger relationship.

Reading

Romans 10:17

Consequently, faith comes from hearing the message, and the message is heard through the word about Christ.

Prayer

Father, I rely on you and what you have to teach me. I want a stronger and better relationship with you, and in my sin I know I sometimes fail to show you that. Father, thank you for your understanding and grace for my sin, and thank you for the offer of relationship you give me. Amen.

Teresa's Notes

Honestly, I'm not perfect about taking time in my Bible every day, and it's one reason I do the work I do. Leading means reading and reading means hope

Personal Response

How do you approach your relationship with God?

We don't need to dedicate large chunks of time to reading and reflecting on the Bible. Reading plans can help us. Take a moment today to locate a reading plan you can use and follow to stay close to the Word, and write down here the one you chose.

Day 19: How to Pray

Devotional

Jesus, in his infinite wisdom, knew that the struggle for prayer is real, honest, and very human. Sometimes, it can be hard to know what to pray for or how we should pray for it, especially when we are deep in pain. Remembering that the Holy Spirit always knows the desires on our heart and acts as the perfect translator on our behalf to God can be comforting. In addition, Jesus gave us a simple and perfect prayer that we can offer up to our Father at any moment in time.

Praying the Lord's prayer not only gives us the right words that we can use at any time and under any conditions, it also helps us focus on what really matters: building the kingdom of God, glorifying our Father, and walking the path that leads us closest to him.

Reading

Matthew 6:9-13

[9]"This, then, is how you should pray:
"'Our Father in heaven,
hallowed be your name,
[10]your kingdom come,
your will be done,
   on earth as it is in heaven.
      [11]Give us today our daily bread.
      [12]And forgive us our debts,
as we also have forgiven our debtors.
      [13]And lead us not into temptation,
but deliver us from the evil one.'

Prayer

Our Father in heaven, hallowed be your name, your
kingdom come, your will be done, on earth as it is in
heaven. Give us today our daily bread. And forgive us our
debts, as we also have forgiven our debtors. And lead us not
into temptation, but deliver us from the evil one. Amen.

Teresa's Notes

On the days I haven't known how to pray, this is where I consistently land. There's a terrific book by Jen Pollock Michel called *Teach Me to Want* and she unpacks this prayer in detail throughout it. Some days, I just focused on the "lead me not into temptation," especially when I was in a particularly severe mood. I think some days that's all we can ask: Lord, just help me manage those temptations.

Personal Response

Read the Lord's prayer three times, each time more carefully and more thoughtfully. Record your reaction and response here. (There are no wrong answers!)

Day 20: Be Steadfast in Prayer

Devotional

Paul reminds us that we are invited into a deep relationship with God, one in which we are invited to share and ask for our heart's deepest desires. As children do not hesitate to tell their parents their needs ("I'm hungry;" "I'm tired;" "My feelings were hurt in school today"), God invites us to do the same with him. Children do not hold back in their requests and in sharing their victories and their challenges. In following their example with God, we embrace a perfect parent-child relationship with him and receive the perfect relational security and love he offers us.

Reading

Ephesians 6:18

And pray in the Spirit on all occasions with all kinds of prayers and requests. With this in mind, be alert and always keep on praying for all the Lord's people.

Prayer

Lord, I am afraid to share with you my deepest worries and desires with you. What if you don't answer me? I worry about feeling disappointed and let down and that holds me back in my relationship with you. Father, help me to break down those walls in my heart that keep me from trusting you honestly and fully. Help me, Father. Amen.

Teresa's Notes

I think it's more the human condition and less my particular flavor of mental illness, but I am known to minimize my role in a situation - especially when I want to put the face on a situation that needs prayer. "God," I might say, "I'm struggling a bit with..." when in reality, I'm a hot mess in that part of my life. If I were to be honest, I would say to him, "God, I'm blowing up this relationship right now and I feel powerless to stop myself." Or, "God, I know I'm being petty about my husband not bringing me flowers today." Worse, I'll pray in praise of him rather than bringing my real hurts and fears to the table. Learning to pray for others has helped me be more honest in my own prayers, and more direct in asking for what I need, too.

Personal Response

What holds you back from taking a childlike response to God?

What is one hurt, challenge, or desire sitting on your heart that you've been afraid to ask him for or trust him with?

What do you think your relationship with God would be like if you were to truly trust him with all your worries, hurts, and longings?

Day 21: All God Wants Is Our Faith

Devotional

As we wrap up this week, we are reminded that all God wants from us is our faith. As we saw with the parable of the mustard seed, he doesn't ask for our perfect faith. What he does demand, we see in the epistle to the Hebrews, is our belief in his existence and the eternal reward he offers his children.

For those who are praying through their "long, dark night" of depression, anxiety, or other mental illness, we have assurance that not only is God still with us, our ability to pray and stay in his word throughout the experience demonstrates tremendous faith and the depth of our longing for true relationship with him.

Reading

Hebrews 11:6

And without faith it is impossible to please God, because anyone who comes to him must believe that he exists and that he rewards those who earnestly seek him.

Prayer

Lord, you offer me a love beyond my comprehension. In any of my human relationships, my illness would cause a separation or hurt the relationship. Instead, you embrace my brokenness and use it to invite me closer to you. It seems to me that my faith is not big enough for you, and yet you tell me it is still enough. I praise you, Lord, for your love and your greatness and I ask that you work the changes in my heart that help me become more worthy of the love you give me. Amen.

Teresa's Notes

I'll be the first to raise my hand and say that sometimes my pride causes me to boast about some of the things I've thought or done in times of weakness or trouble. This reading reminds me that God just shakes his head in those moments and says, "Oh, Teresa, you don't need to do that!" It's frustrating, because I'd like to think that I can manage or control my relationship with him - or at the very least, impress him with the depth and purity of my faith - and the truth is that none of it matters. All he asks for is simple faith.

Personal Response

Have you ever felt separated from God? How did it make you feel?

When you think that God measures our faith only by the fact of it and not the size of it, what is your response?

Week 4:

Looking Beyond

This Season

Overview

No matter the length or the depth of the season we are in, we are assured that our circumstances are temporary. God promises us eternal hope and reminds us that we have a role to play. The Body of Christ is incomplete without each one of us. As you reflect on the readings this week, consider that you are loved and necessary to filling God's plan for all of us.

Day 22: God Promises Us Hope

Devotional

Our reading from Revelations today reminds us that our hope resides in heaven and not on the earth we occupy today. Our circumstances here and now may be difficult, they may be painful, and they may be scary and tough to bear. Whatever they are, they do not change the hope that our loving Father offers us in heaven.

He also offers us hope in his Word. As we learn more about him and his guidebook to life in the Bible, we gain the wisdom to change the circumstances we need to change, to endure the circumstances that cannot be changed, and to live in the hope that he offers us.

Reading

Revelations 21:1-4

[1]Then I saw "a new heaven and a new earth," for the first heaven and the first earth had passed away, and there was no longer any sea. [2]I saw the Holy City, the new Jerusalem, coming down out of heaven from God, prepared as a bride beautifully dressed for her husband. [3]And I heard a loud voice from the throne saying, "Look! God's dwelling place is now among the people, and he will dwell with them. They will be his people, and God himself will be with them and be their God. [4]'He will wipe every tear from their eyes. There will be no more death or mourning or crying or pain, for the old order of things has passed away."

Prayer

Holy and most loving Father, thank you for the hope you offer me. Father, help me gain the wisdom I need so that I move as you desire. Where I should move and make changes, Father, tell me so and grant me strength in the process. If it is your will that I stay in place, Father, help me to endure with patience, love, and faith. Through it all, Lord, help me to remember the hope I have in heaven. Amen.

Teresa's Notes

There was a time when I resigned myself to a life
without romantic love, full of financial instability, and
hoping for basic survival every day. It was ugly: my car was
repossessed twice; I had "pay rent or quit" notices on my
door every month; I learned how to take effective cold
showers; and, I stopped dating altogether. I couldn't imagine
a life for myself where I was financially secure and had love
in my life. If you had pointed me to this reading at that time,
I don't know that I would have believed in the hope
mentioned. Yet, now my response isn't, "Yeah right, that will
never be for me" but "I can hardly wait to see it."

Personal Response

What is one circumstance you live in today that you
need God's guidance on?

List all the possible options and outcomes that you
have. Pray for God's guidance to help you know the right
path to take.

Day 23: This Season Is Temporary

Devotional

When we are in the thick of our suffering, it can be tough to remember that life has seasons. Some seasons are more pleasant than others; some seasons we are just grateful to have survived. Remembering that we are simply in a season and remembering better, or easier, seasons gives us hope to make it through each moment and each day when our struggles are the most challenging.

Ultimately, we live not for this world but for the next. God uses each moment of our lives for his glory even when we can't see it or don't understand it. Our existence on this world is temporary and helps form and prepare us for the wonders that he has prepared for us in Heaven. Our loving Father promises us a perfect experience in eternal life. Even when we struggle to hold on to hope in a difficult season in life, we can take hope in the eternal life he promises.

Note: Romans 8 is an excellent resource for exploring this topic further and in more depth.

Reading

2 Corinthians 4:16-18

[16]Therefore we do not lose heart. Though outwardly we are wasting away, yet inwardly we are being renewed day by day. [17]For our light and momentary troubles are achieving for us an eternal glory that far outweighs them all. [18]So we fix our eyes not on what is seen, but on what is unseen, since what is seen is temporary, but what is unseen is eternal.

Prayer

Father, this season of suffering has gone on too long and I pray for its end. Even as I pray, Father, I know that you are using my pain for your good to build your kingdom. Lord, let my trials be a testimony and grant comfort to someone else in pain. Help me remember that this season, too, shall pass. I take hope and comfort in the eternal life you promise me and I know the depths of my suffering will pale in comparison to the glory that is Heaven. Amen.

Teresa's Notes

One of the first things I learned as a Christian was the idea of "seasons in life." I love this idea because it reminds me that everything is temporary. A season of joy is as temporary as a season of pain. When I got my diagnosis and started the healing process, my seasons shortened. One week was full of despair and the next was full of hope. Through it all, and directly related to the work I was doing, my inner self was restored. As I've healed, my seasons lengthened to match what more people experience. In addition, I can handle my tough seasons better and savor my joyous seasons more. I have more capacity for the emotions they bring.

Personal Response

What makes it difficult to remember that pain is simply a temporary season in your life?

What gives you hope when you are in your darkest and most difficult moments?

Day 24: There Is a Purpose to Your Trial

Devotional

Jesus did many acts that others around him did not comprehend. They didn't understand that not everything he did was for them to understand; in some cases, the acts were simply witnesses to the power, might, and benevolence of our loving father. Often, those touched by what Jesus did and the friendship he offered were several steps removed from him and the apostles; they simply heard the stories of what he did and believed.

In the same way, we often do not see how our lives or experiences serve God's plan. We assume that we are the ones to gain or learn from our experiences and that is not always the case. Sometimes, the simple truth of our endurance is testimony for others. Sometimes, we aren't the ones who tell the stories of our faith and experiences. Others witness what we live through and share our stories to give hope to others who find themselves in similar circumstances.

It is often a comfort to know that our experiences serve God's greater plan and we simply trust in Him to work our circumstances out for good. He reminds us of this simple Biblical truth in Romans 8:28: *And we know that in all things God works for the good of those who love him, who have been called according to his purpose.*

Reading

John 13:7

Jesus replied, "You do not realize now what I am doing, but later you will understand."

Prayer

Lord, it is incredibly difficult to remember that my sufferings fulfill your plan. I wish I could see the entirety of your plan and know how my pain enables its success. Even so, Father, I trust that you are using this experience for your good, to help someone else in the Body of Christ or as a witness to someone you are pursuing. Grant me comfort and ease my burden, Lord, and let my story be the witness you desire. Amen.

Teresa's Notes

"But why would God do this to me if he loves me so much?" It's a question that every Christian grapples with at least once in their spiritual walk; none of us have easy lives. I can't answer for you, but now I can answer for me: out of my experiences, I've found my purpose. I would not be able to do this ministry or write this devotional if I did not live with my diagnosis. I know others have found that their trials did not lead them to their purpose but aided them in it. I know that my purpose is not your purpose. I know that I can't give you an answer that satisfies you deep in your soul; at some point, we take it on faith that our trials and tribulations have a bigger purpose behind them. What I can do is point you to this verse and say that Jesus mystified people even before his crucifixion.

Personal Response

What is one story you've been told of someone else's experience, difficulties, or sufferings? Who told it to you? How did it impact you?

When you think of your own story bearing witness to God, his glory, and his kingdom, what is your reaction? Why?

Day 25: You Are God's Handiwork

Devotional

We are not accidents! As we discussed in the first week of this devotional, you are God's beloved. You weren't a test copy or an experiment: he made you, he *designed* you with a purpose in mind.

The word "handiwork" can also be translated as "workmanship." When we think of workmanship, we often think of a master craftsman: one who knows his trade so deeply and so expertly that we can only marvel at the creations that come from his hands. If human craftsmen leave us speechless, how much more awe-inspiring are God's creations - like you?

Not only are we made incredibly, we are made to do God's works, works he planned *in advance* for us to do. We have a role to play and we are designed and made perfectly to play it by the most expert craftsman to ever exist.

Reading

Ephesians 2:10

For we are God's handiwork, created in Christ Jesus to do good works, which God prepared in advance for us to do.

Prayer

Lord, it awes me to consider that I am a creation at your hand. You are the perfect craftsman, and I am your creation. Your perfect creation, designed and made as you desired and as you planned. It makes me realize that I am not worthless or incompetent in your eyes, Father. I am made for something greater than these circumstances and I praise you for it. Amen.

Teresa's Notes

My small group and I did a study on spiritual gifts (by Chip Ingram; I recommend checking it out) while I was first learning how to manage my depression. The idea that I was made for something bigger, that I was *designed* to do something specific was new to me. It also meant that my responsibility wasn't "to follow my bliss" but to uncover the good works that God planned in advance for me to do. It was a shift in perspective for me that made me feel significant and important. The answer didn't come that summer; I spent significant time trying and discarding different ideas before I realized the path God was leading me down. Truthfully, I know that I'm still not operating 100% within my purpose, but I am confident that I'm getting closer every day.

Personal Response

Have you considered that you are made just as intended? What does it mean to you?

Our acts do not and cannot wipe away the perfection created by the master craftsman. What is one way you can reflect back the love and gratitude you have for him today?

You were made in advance to do the "good works" God planned for you. What does this statement mean to you?

Day 26: You Are a New Creation

Devotional

Often, in our illness, we commit acts that cause others pain and damage the relationships we hold most valuable. Even after we ask and receive forgiveness from God and the people we hurt, it is common to still feel guilt. Guilt left unaddressed ferments into shame.

When we offer our hurts and surface our ill deeds to God and beg his forgiveness, his grace covers us. No matter the deed, no matter the shame, he offers us truly unconditional love and grace. When we hold on to shame and guilt after receiving God's grace, we are really saying that our sin is bigger than God. We say that we know better than God, that if he *really knew* what we'd done, he would not forgive us. When we look at it from this light, we realize how absurd our attitude is. Our God is great, magnificent, and deeply loving.

When we accept Christ, as our Lord and Savior, not only are we adopted into the family of Christ, we are made a new creation. Like Paul, we cast off the sins we've committed and dedicate ourselves to fulfilling our role in God's plan. We ask God's forgiveness and accept the grace he offers, knowing that his grace is bigger than our sins and his grace covers all - unconditionally.

Take heart in being his new creation. Take heart that he is working tremendous changes in your life and in your heart. You are a new creation.

Reading

2Corinthians 5:17

Therefore, if anyone is in Christ, the new creation has come: The old has gone, the new is here!

Prayer

Father, today I ask your forgiveness for not accepting the grace and forgiveness you offer me. Your mercy is great, oh Lord! Lord, I am excited to see the creation you are making in me and I embrace the plans you have for me. I turn my guilt and shame over to you, Father, in praise for your son, whose perfect sacrifice wipes away all my sins. All my sins, Father. Even the idea overwhelms me. I praise you; I thank you; I give you glory for your mercy, your kindness, and your amazing grace. Amen.

Teresa's Notes

When my psychiatrist first uttered the words "you have bipolar disorder," it was a relief for me. As he explained the symptoms and their common results, I realized that he was reading pages out of the book of my life. Suddenly, many of the decisions and choices I'd made had explanations behind them; I felt loads of shame fall of my shoulders. In fact, the words "I am unchained and unbound" greeted me every morning for several months after my diagnosis. If you ask me, I've experienced resurrection-in-life. If God were to deny me the eternal resurrection, I would be disappointed but not angry: I've already tasted a new life and it is enough for me.

Personal Response

What is one sin you've considered unforgivable in your heart? Have you asked God for his forgiveness and grace?

How do you feel after turning over a sin to God? What holds you back from releasing yourself from guilt or shame over it?

Day 27: The Body of Christ Needs You

Devotional

Just as it may be difficult to see God's plan for our life, we can be struck by feelings of worthlessness, incompetence and fear. We may remember that we are God's child and still forget that we have a role to play in the Body of Christ.

Paul reminds us that the Body of Christ does not walk as well as it does when it is whole. In the same way, the Body of Christ does not fulfill its mission here on earth when we do not step into the role God designed for us. The job may be small, such as greeting people at church on Sundays, or it may be large, such as moving countries and doing mission work in a foreign land in a foreign language. Whatever the mission God has planned for you, you are the only one who can fulfill it. The Body of Christ needs you in it.

Reading

1 Corinthians 12:12-23a

[12]Just as a body, though one, has many parts, but all its many parts form one body, so it is with Christ. [13]For we were all baptized by one Spirit so as to form one body - whether Jews or Gentiles, slave or free - and we were all given the one Spirit to drink. [14]Even so the body is not made up of one part but of many.

[15]Now if the foot should say, "Because I am not a hand, I do not belong to the body," it would not for that reason stop being part of the body. [16]And if the ear should say, "Because I am not an eye, I do not belong to the body," it would not for that reason stop being part of the body. [17]If the whole body were an eye, where would the sense of hearing be? If the whole body were an ear, where would the sense of smell be? [18]But in fact God has placed the parts in the body, every one of them, just as he wanted them to be. [19]If they were all one part, where would the body be? [20]As it is, there are many parts, but one body.

[21]The eye cannot say to the hand, "I don't need you!" And the head cannot say to the feet, "I don't need you!" [22]On the contrary, those parts of the body that seem to be weaker are indispensable, [23]and the parts that we think are less honorable we treat with special honor.

Prayer

Lord, I want to be your vessel. I want to fulfill the mission you have for me. It can be so hard, Father, when I don't have energy or feel worthless. Help me know and use the gifts you created in me. Don't let me rest until I am working on the mission you designed for me. Have patience with me as I get started on this road and uncover the mission you have for me in this season of my life. Set my soul on fire for you, Lord. Amen.

Teresa's Notes

I grew up being told "what a leader" I was. It was tremendous pressure, especially because it seemed that every time I attempted to lead there were disastrous consequences. It was frustrating and defeating. When we did the spiritual gifts study, then, it was a surprise for me to realize that I wasn't designed to be a leader! I am an encourager at heart, and encouragers often look like leaders. Now, pair up that idea with today's reading and the sense of relief I felt was incredible. I'm not responsible for being the brain of the Body of Christ; I might be a fingernail. Fingernails are still important (just ask anyone who's ripped one off) and they play an entirely different role for the body than the brain does. I may not be responsible for keeping the entire organism moving, but my role is still important.

Personal Response

It can be overwhelming to figure out where to start or how to figure out what God's purpose for us is. Start by reaching out to one of the leaders of your church and ask for ways you can help. The first role may not be the right role, and that's OK. Simply taking that first step gets you moving on the path to uncovering God's vision for your mission.

Who can you call today? What holds you back from making that call?

Day 28: Shine Your Light Brightly

Devotional

Knowing that we are fearfully and wonderfully made, designed in advance for the good works God has planned for us, and understanding that there is a role in the Body of Christ that only we can fill, Jesus reminds us that we are to shine our light onto the world. Our light is merely a reflection of his, and in allowing our light to shine, we share the hope and love that his light represents and glorify our God in Heaven, who is worthy of all praise.

Reading

Matthew 5:14-16

[14]"You are the light of the world. A town built on a hill cannot be hidden. [15]Neither do people light a lamp and put it under a bowl. Instead they put it on its stand, and it gives light to everyone in the house. [16]In the same way, let your light shine before others, that they may see your good deeds and glorify your Father in heaven.

Prayer

Lord, the idea of shining my light is scary. It means being seen and that intimidates me. Yet, Lord, how can I hide you from the world? I ask that your light shine so strongly in me that it overcomes my fear and timidity. I do not ask this so that others may see me, Lord, but that they may see you and the great works you have done in me and in my brothers and sisters in Christ. Amen.

Teresa's Notes

On the scale of scary ideas, letting my light shine was near the top when I was in the depth of my disorder. I didn't want attention; it was uncomfortable to be seen. Now, having received the healing and improved life that I have, I feel an urge to let people know that it's possible and to share my story with them. Ultimately, my story isn't about me and what I've done; it's about how God has worked through my life to get me to this incredibly joyful place.

You may not be where I am yet, and that's OK; my miracle took years. Even so, remember that you are special, powerful, and significant, and in letting your light shine, you add something important and special to the world that only you can offer. Baby steps may be all you can offer at this point; I'll bet your baby steps are bigger than mine were (I was pretty afraid). Just remember that even the tiniest step is important and valuable.

Personal Response

What does it mean to let your light shine?

What holds you back from putting your lamp on a table for all to see?

What is one message you can hold on to that will give you courage when fear overtakes you?

Next Steps

Congratulations on finishing this devotional! You may be wondering what's next and I'd like to share some options with you.

- Depending on where you are in your mental health journey and spiritual walk, you may want to simply start back in on this devotional and read it again.

- Joining my warm and welcoming Facebook group at Wounded Birds Ministry for Mental Health for ongoing support, education, and encouragement.

- Joining or starting a mental health support group in your area. You can find one by searching either the Mental Health Grace Alliance website (mentalhealthgracealliance.org) or the National Alliance on Mental Illness site (nami.org) Starting a group is simple also; just let your local church know that you are interested in offering one and they will typically work with you to order books, etc.

- Joining a small group (some churches call them "Bible studies" or "home groups") through your local church. If you don't currently belong to a church (or aren't a Christian), that's OK. A good church will help you find a group that's right for you and meets you where you are.

- Talking with a pastor or church leader about some options for volunteering or assisting at your local church. Your first opportunity may not be the right one for you (I went through several before landing where I belonged), but give each role a few months and a serious go before considering a change.

Finally, if this devotional touched you in any way or if you have questions or comments, I would love to hear from you at teresa@woundedbirdsministry.com.

May God bless you as you walk your road. Amen.

Acknowledgments

As with most books, this one only has one name on the cover. Also like most books, this one would not have come into being without the loving support of many others.

First of all, my deepest thanks go to God, Jesus, and the Holy Spirit for guiding and supporting me through this process. I pray that I've listened properly and that this book is what you desired. There have been several cases of divine intervention along the road to publishing this book, and I am grateful for all of them.

I also want to thank Sherry Atkinson and Cynthia Darden of Crystal Prairie Media. You held my hand through each step of the process, encouraging me along the way. There is no way this book would exist without your assistance.

Thanks also go to my beta readers and prayer warriors. Summer and Karen, I appreciate your willingness to take a month of your lives and dedicate it to this venture. Your feedback has made this devotional stronger.

I am grateful to Pastor Chris Martinez and Dana Nolen, whose theological feedback helped me tremendously. A devotional that leads people astray is no good at all, and I appreciate your candor and assistance.

I would be remiss if I didn't mention Sirsey Martinez and Brian Bensing, both professional Christian counselors who stepped in with advice to make sure that this devotional is encouraging and inviting. I am in awe of what you two do on a daily basis, and I am grateful for your support here.

To my Southwinds Church family, to my small groups, my family, and to everyone who has been praying along the way: Wow. There are no words to express how you have lifted me up in the moments I've struggled. Most of the passages in this devotional come from suggestions I've received from my faith community, and you have given me strength in some of my weakest and darkest moments. You teach me daily what it means to belong to a community, what healthy relationships look and feel like, and how we support and love each other in good times and in bad.

And, of course, to my husband. Living with someone with a bipolar disorder is not easy, and you handle it with grace and love. It's pretty interesting that you married an avowed non-Christian and now have a wife who wrote a devotional, isn't it? God's plans are bigger than we are, and he knew what he was doing when he put you in my life. "*Ya yo sé.*"

One last acknowledgment: You, the reader. Seasons of pain and anguish are tough at best. I know how hard you fight every day. I know that some days are better than other days. I know that sometimes, it doesn't seem like it can get better. I hope you know now how loved and important you are. The body of Christ needs you, and I pray for you every day.

CPSIA information can be obtained
at www.ICGtesting.com
Printed in the USA
LVHW040039210519
618568LV00017B/264

9 780692 114148